*THE CHRONICLES
OF A MORTAL
IN ARCADIA*

THE
Chronicles of a Mortal
IN
Arcadia

a fictionalized memoir in verse by

R. CLIFT

The Chronicles of a Mortal in Arcadia
Copyright © 2024 by Rachel Clift.

All rights reserved. This book or any portion thereof may not be reproduced or used in any manner whatsoever without the express written permission of the author except for the use of brief quotations in the context of reviews.

ISBN: 978-1-960045-05-8 (paperback),
978-1-960045-04-1 (hardcover).

Written at Château d'Orquevaux Artist Residency in July 2023.
Book design & layout by Rachel Clift.
Cover Art: *Summer* (1890) by Thomas Wilmer Dewing.
Interior Illustrations by Aquarellina, Beigetime, NatashaKun ArtCreationsDesign, SensualArt, Christina Li.

First printing edition, 2024.

@r.cliftpoetry
rcliftpoetry.com
Rachel Clift

*For the Artists who saw me as a true poet
& the time when that was enough*

ALSO BY R. CLIFT

TO FEEL ANYTHING AT ALL
TO BE REMEMBERED
TOMORROW WILL BE KINDER

UNTIL WE MEET AGAIN
YOUR THOUGHTS DESERVE A DECENT PLACE TO LIVE
THE POETRY OF WILDFLOWERS: FIELD JOURNAL
BEAUTY EXISTS SO CLOSE TO AGONY
VOICES IN GIANT CITIES

UNSENT LOVE LETTERS: AN ANTHOLOGY OF WORDS LEFT UNSPOKEN
THE ART & POETRY OF TRAVELERS: VOL I

Contents

A Note from the Author........................ vii
Prologue xiii

1. Mere Mortality............................... 1
2. Arcadian Days................................ 9
    The God that Sees Me...................... 11
3. The Company of the Divine................... 17
4. To Create is to Remember.................... 35
    The Gods that Question Me................. 40
5. Hesitation & Doubt.......................... 47
    The Rules of Arcadia...................... 53
6. Elysian Fields.............................. 55
    The Curse of the Gods..................... 59
7. Human & Ephermal............................ 67
8/9. Arcadian Nights........................... 81
    The Goddess that Knows Me................. 89
10. Intrinsicality............................ 101
11. The Immortals............................. 115
12. Of the Soul............................... 141
13. Prophecies................................ 147

Epilogue 163
Sketchbook 165
Acknowledgments 173
Glossary of Gods 175
About the Author 179

A Note from the Author

This is a true story told through the lens of vivid imagination. In July of 2023 I arrived at the Château d'Orquevaux— a centuries old manor house nestled away in the countryside of north-eastern France. In a village with a population of well under 100 people, no businesses, no cafes, no shops— I felt like I was existing in an world outside our own. For a few weeks, the only thing I needed to be was a poet. It was like a dream. In fact, on our first night, a painter named Erin smiled and said, *it feels like we're in heaven.*

That shared notion is what sparked the idea for this book. I couldn't help but think— well— what if we *were* in heaven, paradise— or at least the mythological version of it— *Arcadia*. I desperately wanted to capture as much of my experience as possible— but to tell the story in a fantastical way. So, my imagination took hold. In my head, all of the artists I lived with had two names. Their actual name, and the name of the forgotten god I chose for them upon first impression.

For two weeks I kept this project a secret. No one but my sister knew I was writing a collection based on the residency, based on the people around me. I never anticipated I'd fill a journal and a half with over 250 poems. The inspiration was non-stop, and I've never experienced anything like it before.

In our final days together, I revealed what I had been working on and shared some of these poems with the artists and chateau staff. I told them of their Immortal counterparts and reveled in their suprise and smiles. Only they will know precisely who is who— which is just how I envisioned it. These poems are for them, after all. Every last word.

Each chapter represents a single day, and at times they started to blur together— hence chapter 8/9. I cherish this collection dearly to remember each hour. And that's what this memoir is. Pages of memories— of the tiniest moments that would've otherwise been forgotten. If that's all this book is, then that is enough for me. But if it can be more— I do hope you will resonate with this chronicle of a lost thing who finds herself on quite the unexpected journey of acceptance. Whether you consider yourself an artist or not— may you, too, accept yourself for all that you are, and may that lift you higher— as if you had wings.

Rachel Clift
January, 2024

Poems

Prologue

The curious Aurai follow close behind
and it seems as though
time itself
is frozen
in anticipation
as I inch closer
to this new chapter.

Wading through
a vast field of golden stars
surrounding the outer bounds
of Arcadia, there is not
a single bloom facing
towards me— instead,
they turn towards
the very direction I am headed—
which is to say, *this way to the light,
keep going— follow like a winged thing
to a bright flame and know that soon—
you will be seen clearly
for who you are.*

CHAPTER ONE

Mere Mortality

The mythology you've been told
is somewhat wrong— for many of
the Titans— the old gods—
are no longer imprisoned
in Tartarus (foolish Zeus
only thinks that's true)
but are living freely— deep
within the heart of Arcadia—
in a place called Chateau Rouge.

Mortals are rarely
allowed here— and I
was only invited by
the kind blessing
of a Naiad.
I have traveled
all this way to learn
from those who
dwell here in hopes

The Chronicles of a Mortal in Arcadia

of earning my own
artist's immortality.

Yet, at the gate I can't help
but stop and think—
are my words
even worthy?

The chateau perches
on the hillside like
Dionysus on his throne—
overlooking rolling green hills,
a lake filled with dark and
mysterious secrets, and a stone
village far below.

This monarch is a gentle
ruler— more butterfly
than brute. Wispy clouds
hover above and an open door
invites me in.

The Immortals are in the salon
and I'm in just the other room—
out of sight from the doorway
and windows— and no one has
noticed— because why would they?
I've barely introduced myself and
I only know a handful of names—

Mere Mortality

I know— I'm sure— (I hope) in just
a matter of days— if I'm ever gone this long,
a friendly face will pop their head in (and by
this time I'll know their name as if it were my own)
to check in on me and deliver a hot cup of tea.

Dionysus speaks and the room falls silent
for the first time since I arrived.
Gods of old surround me. Creators,
painters, sculptors, writers, and poets
all turn their heads (and hearts) to listen.
Dionysus speaks and we smile. Dionysus
speaks and we laugh. Dionysus speaks and
we feel at home. At this moment— they
may all be strangers— but when I look
around the room— I have the most
intense feeling that in some far-off
lifetime— I've known them all before.

This must have been what Versailles
was like before the mortal Sun King melted down
all the stars in the heavens to create his
gilded palace. A quiet hunting lodge
not inhabited by noble lords and ladies—
but overtaken by Artists, *Immortals*.

In this place, you will not find perfectly polished silver
or stiff brocade curtains— you will find mismatched
velvet couches, old wooden tables covered in

paint splatters— you will find every window
wide open (with no curtains at all)
to invite in the brisk morning breeze,
the butterflies and honey bees.

You will not find precious gems and jewels
but you will see more sparkling wildflowers
than you ever thought possible. Topaz, amethyst,
sapphire, diamond, ruby-adorned blooms turn up
their little faces to greet you as you wander past—
searching for acceptance into this otherworldly place.

And when you happen upon wisteria blooming you can
almost hear the flowers themselves whisper,
Welcome, fair stranger.

Theia, goddess of sight and shining
light— the one with fire in her hair
looks right through me as if she can see
all my years (even the ones I've yet to live).

She tells me how we need those
who walk around without their skin
and I want to believe in the thought
that vulnerability is the better
option for me but it's hard
when it hurts so much.

In the same breath, she tells me of
its burden, how hard it must be
to live one's life with the heart

Mere Mortality

on the outside of the body and
it was at this moment I felt seen—
from the inside out— and for a
brief second— I had a glimpse
at what it must feel like
to belong.

Wine bottles surround us,
some half-empty, most
barely hanging on
to their last drops—
the Immortals gather
around a large wooden
table in the cool cellars—
as I imagine they have
for centuries.

*When the sun goes down
we go underground.*

There is much noise here
and overlapping conversations—
an underlying heartbeat
of music and beyond that—
silence of those rolling hills
and wild forests fast asleep.

The Immortals cheer
when fresh bread is
brought down by Helios
and I am reminded
of the simple joy of existing.

The Chronicles of a Mortal in Arcadia

There is a thrill here
that cannot be found
when swimming in deep
waters or standing on
mountaintops— a thrill
of connection— or perhaps
reconnection— of meeting
once more in this old cellar—
where creatures have
gathered and met
for many years passed and
decades to come.

Soon from now—
in my seat, there will
be someone else—
and I suppose
that's only fair.

There is a monster
living in the attic room
and I think the old
wardrobe is haunted too.

Daphne tells me it has
crawled up from Hades
to lay claim to this
earthly domain.

There are devils
to be found around

Mere Mortality

*every corner— and
on rare occasions—
they find their way
into heaven.*

I think of banishing
this demon— but
instead— I let it stay.

It's true after all— all
demons once were angels
and maybe this one
is just trying to find
its way back home.

CHAPTER TWO

Arcadian Days

I hear the bell ring— dawn sweeps
over the valley— and I fly out
the garden door to join
the swifts— or sparrows—
(I always get the two confused)
with an apricot between my teeth,
I trot through the village—
trying not to get too distracted
by the ivy-covered windows
or the old red post box or the
wilting pink roses.

There are chocolate pastries to taste—
and I hope they've saved me one.

———◆———

Legend has it— Chateau Rouge
used to be a dull, beige stone—

The Chronicles of a Mortal in Arcadia

until Dionysus brought
the Immortals to live here
and capture its beauty.

Now, after centuries
of attention— of epic love poems
and intimate paintings—
the walls are ever blushing.

There is lightning
in the cellar of
the estate—
stolen from Zeus,
as the story goes, and it
has been harnessed to power
all the stars caught in
the chandeliers of
the floors above.

*Don't touch that
or it will kill you,*
Rhea tells me
as we walk through
the underground tunnels
beneath the dining hall—
I can't help but wonder
what other dangers lie here.

THE GOD THAT SEES ME

I have crossed the
rickety wooden bridge
to the floating island—
a gold dusting of flowers
cover the ground beneath
one of the sentry pine trees.
I approach this ancient god
and he tries to speak to me—
but I do not know his language.

I walk closer to see that at one time
he must have held fire in his core—
maybe even lightning.

The black charring scars stain
his insides like India ink—
this makes me wonder even more
what he is trying to tell me.

So I take another step forward
and what I hear must be true—
a sharp, deep, creaking voice saying
I can see your scars too.

The Chronicles of a Mortal in Arcadia

This god is covered in vines—
but I don't think she minds.

She carefully dips one branch
into the lake— just to assure
the timid waters that
she is still there, watching
over the village in silent affection.

Her needles are soft, like
the gentle hand of a mother—
she sways as if rocking
her little pine blooms to sleep
and I can't help but feel at ease
in the quiet embrace of her limbs.

Her roots reach out— through
the heart of the floating island—
wrapping around her lover
and helping him to stand—
keeping just enough strength
for herself— and giving the rest
to the land.

———◇———

As I walk the clover path
from the old gods to the
waterfall I hear footsteps
crackling in the forest
beside me— I turn
my head and peer
through the trees—

Arcadian Days

nothing. Another step
forward— the footsteps again!

I turn my head— nothing—
I turn away and hear
the beating of wings.

The nymphs must be teasing me.

I drop an angel feather
in the River Styx and now
all the souls are restless.

Ripples dance through the water
and I watch as the feather skims
across the top— attracting even
the darkest souls to the surface.

One has a gold shimmering
in its scales— and I wonder
if that light is coming from within—
or if it is simply a reflection.

When I consider my own soul—
I wonder the same thing.

The Chronicles of a Mortal in Arcadia

Every night there is a feast—
we are in the company
of Dionysus after all.

His trusted demi-gods and
maenads spend hours
preparing each meal with
the utmost care— I stumble
through their language
to learn their names and
thank them the best I can.

After piling my plate, I settle
in among the Immortals and
the room remains at a constant
hum of conversation.

I'm not sure what to say, so I focus
on my vegetable quiche until
Lelantos asks me a question—
then I look up to see everyone
at the table waiting for me to speak.

CHAPTER THREE

The Company of the Divine

The estate has
a towering gateway
with gold spires,
stone columns,
and one particular
defining feature—

the gate
is always
open.

The Immortals are once more
in the dining hall
and I sit at the furthest table
away
from the morning sun.
I'm a winter's child, you see—

The Chronicles of a Mortal in Arcadia

and I've always been more drawn
to the cool shadows. I do not
feel quite brave enough
to sit in a spotlight.

So I leave my favorite book
with Lelantos (I hope he
enjoys the text) and follow
the little griffin to the kitchen.

I overhear Circe
from across the room—
she's planning to
harness the elements.

Earth, fire, air, water— to capture
them as her own. A book of magic,
she has referenced— to teach herself
more about the primordial deities.

It must be made aware, however,
she does not intend to trap them
for selfish use— but to capture
their essence and set them free—

to share their magnificence
with the mortal realm.

The Company of the Divine

I've yet to see
Morpheus this
morning and I
suppose he's still
in the land of
dreams.

———◇———

Eris runs by
with a whole
cafetière full
of ambrosia
and four books
spilling from
her pen— she
stops for a
moment to
ask my name
and when I tell
her of all the things
I want to create
in this life,
she looks at me
with a sly smile
and a flame
in her eye—
saying,
*You must be
as delusional
as I am.*

The Chronicles of a Mortal in Arcadia

A little orange griffin
lives on the estate— and
some may say he owns
the place. (I think
Rhea would agree.)

He greets me each morning
and follows me from the
gatehouse to the front door.

When I feel extra
out of place,
he finds me
and snuggles
into my arms—

helping my heart beat
slower and a grin to
find my face again.

I fly down the hill
to meet Cadmus
at the gatehouse—

the Immortals are waiting
with pens in their hands
and paper in their laps.

Our teacher's voice fills the room
as he tells us to capture
the hidden places in our minds.

The Company of the Divine

Bring them out of
the shadows and
into the light—
cast them in ink
for everyone to see.

Share your secrets—
he says— and you will
know yourself better.

You may not know this—
but the River Styx runs
right through Arcadia—
Demeter made sure of it.

The souls come here
to feel the sun's rays
through the surface
and hear the music
of the waterfalls.

And if you look around,
you will not see a desolate
body of water— you will see
the Naiads dancing along the surface—
so many of them— the ripples
look like rain.

Aurai fly higher and tease
their watery sisters as they
bounce off their shoulders.

The Chronicles of a Mortal in Arcadia

The flower nymphs— Anthousai—
lounge by the banks in
more vivid colors than
you've ever known and
onyx-feathered birds with
alabaster beaks raise their
young between the willow trees.

When it comes to sharing stories
of where souls spend eternity—
classic mythology has lied.

I am here to tell you—
the River Styx is alive.

I cross the broken bridge
by Charon's harbor and settle down
by a rushing waterfall.

I sing to the souls of Styx
and they gather below to listen.
The Aurai flutter above—
resting on the algae that has gathered
at the banks. I notice one nymph
is caught in a spider web— so I
reach down to offer her my hand.

She wraps her feathery fingers
around my thumb. I hold my palm up
to the heavens and she leaps—
catching the wind towards the horizon.

I watch until she fades from view—
she didn't bother saying thank you.

———◇———

Eros flies by
at the heels
of Hermes
and I try
to catch his
attention—

his long hair
messy from
flight— but
it's no use—

I can't even
glimpse his eyes.

———◇———

Andromeda's caverns
are quiet in midday—
still as a heart that has
just stopped beating.

I wander the dark corridors
and discover the stones
chill the bottoms of my feet
as if I were walking on snow.

I feel at home here— in a way—

The Chronicles of a Mortal in Arcadia

my frost-covered soul
fits right in with the cold.

———◇———

I stumble upon Asteria
resting in the caverns—
she always has a
slight glow about her—
as if the stars fling themselves
from the heavens just to be near her.

I ask her if she's seen the monster
that lurks within the caves
and she shakes her head—
unafraid. *I've taken on Scorpius
and Hydra head-on in the southern sky—
you have nothing to fear. I promise—
dear mortal— you are safe here.*

———◇———

I bathe in the grotto of sirens
and the water is as warm as
this midsummer day.

For a moment I feel
a breath of immortality—
as if all my fears are washed away.

The Company of the Divine

I return to the chateau
by the path of the willows—
holding hands with
each of the young gods
before continuing on.
The sirens are watching me—
but every time I turn my head
to the lake— all I see are ripples
of what (or who) was there.

The muses are meditating
in the garden— eyes closed—
beneath a shelter of swaying branches.

I watch from afar— too nervous
to join them. I feel— so intensely—
the shortcomings of my mortality.

Who am I to be in the company of the divine?

The smallest willow
is tied to the ground—
he must have kept
wandering off.

The Chronicles of a Mortal in Arcadia

This secret path
was crafted
by Artemis herself—
two proud stags
guard the entrance—

I'm not entirely sure
where it leads—

but I take a step
forward, regardless,
and they allow me to pass.

I find Morpheus by the gate—
music surrounds him like
a mist and follows him
wherever he goes.

His eyes are hidden from me,
but when I approach—
he smiles. He has conjured
a floating chessboard and asks me
to play— I politely decline—
not knowing what would happen
if I were to lose to the god of dreams.

The Company of the Divine

A nymph has perished—
laying on her back,
wings motionless,
body lifeless.

Daphne mourns
and I collect her
corpse from the
pathway. I carefully
give her to the open
hands of Morpheus—

who releases her soul
into the air
(where she was
always meant to be)

and buries her
corporeal self
beneath a canopy
of Queen Anne's lace—

where she may rest
comfortably.

The home of Charon
is covered in
barren vines
and webs woven
between them—

inside it is dark
and motionless—

but it doesn't feel
threatening— it feels
lonely.

I have met
the mother of
the willows—

an ancient goddess
residing by a pool
with the nymphs—

her thick branches
protecting them
from the voyeuristic
gaze of the satyrs.

The bells
of the evening
hour are ringing
as I sneak by the satyrs—
attempting to avoid
detection.

Selene warned me
of their poor manners.

The Company of the Divine

The Immortals
will be gathering soon—
so I sit outside
by the front door
(that is perpetually
wide open at this
time of night)

and I wait.

He shows me shining steel trees
with copper leaves— each one
hand-made and engraved.

From the branches— tiny
silver acorns hang from the
smallest limbs and when
the breezes blow through—
they ring like bells.

I stand in a forest created
by the hands of one man.

I ask him why and he tells me
how he has always longed
for something meaningful to hold.

There are entire realms in his mind
that he wants to bring to life—
and what I've realized, what was
never told to me in the legends of old—

The Chronicles of a Mortal in Arcadia

the world that Atlas carries on his shoulders
is one of his own careful making.

Selene and Asteria
wander away at dusk
and I don't see them again
until the middle of the night—
when I happen to look up
at the sky and there they are—
sparkling in the heavens and
half-hidden in the phases
of the new moon.

Still— they seem
so much more at home
way out there on their own.

I follow the sound of laughter
into the tunnels and caves
below the estate.
The steps wind down
as if I'm descending
some sort of timeworn tower
and the voices grow louder.

The Immortals are circled
around the table with wine bottles
scattered between them once again.

The Company of the Divine

They are conjuring strange creatures
into existence and Gaia invites me to join.

I don't have a particular talent for much
beyond the written word, but I don't dare
to refuse a primordial. At the table— I am
welcomed as one of their own.

For a moment it feels
as if the minutes
have stopped passing—
and I wonder if one of them
has altered time.

Eris is powerful— and she knows it.
I would be lying if I said
I wasn't intimidated.

I don't quite understand her,
yet, but I know there's
so much more.

Her exterior is hard
and a bit sharp (which
I think she's proud of)
and at times, I wish I had
a little more of that.

She is the daughter
of night— you see—
and although she tends

to release chaos into
every room she enters—
she doesn't apologize.

She doesn't say sorry
for who she is— and
I find that as equally
impressive and as I do
unfathomable.

Nike, with her feathered wings
tightly tucked behind her, almost hidden,
peers at me from across the room
and I wonder what she sees.

Can she tell I don't belong?
I wonder if I should leave.

It's too presumptuous to assume
I know anything at all from
a simple glance. Perhaps she
was staring past me. Perhaps
I didn't even cross her mind.

How silly of me—
to think I matter that much.

CHAPTER FOUR

To Create is to Remember

The morning air carried
by Zephyr's winds
has brought a chill in with it
from the mountains
and all the sparrows are singing.

It has been said that birds cry out
each morning to assure their loved ones
that they've made it through the night.

Maybe we are not so different— and
that's why we sing too— why we leave
pieces of ourselves behind in art—
it is a way of saying,

I'm alive. I made it. I'm still here.

So please— know that when I say
IMMORTALS, what I truly mean is *ARTISTS*.

The Chronicles of a Mortal in Arcadia

I borrow a lyre from the muses—
teaching myself to play— one chord
at a time. It's been so long since I've
written a song, but I at least want to try.

The tough strings dig into my fingertips
and they start to throb and turn raw—
even now, while holding this pen— they ache.

Creation has never been a simple thing—
the Immortals tell me— and there is always
a price to pay.

———◇———

It is raining in Arcadia
and the Immortals fill
the rooms of the chateau—
they are all artisans, you see,
spending their days crafting
their own immortality in
oil pastels and metalwork
and written word.

If you think eternity is
just given away freely—
that is not the case.

To create is to remember— and
it is up to each artist to render
something new and sincere—
each and every day— in order
to remain everlasting.

To Create is to Remember

The hands of Eos
are covered in
turquoise blue
from painting
the dawn
this morning.

Lelantos is just in
the other room and
I had no clue until
I heard his voice through
the walls— I suppose
he truly does
have a talent for
invisibility.

It's uncanny and almost
ironic- how the Immortal
known as "the unseen one"
cares the most about
making others feel seen.

The Chronicles of a Mortal in Arcadia

Morpheus appears
around midday—
only able to leave
the dream world
once everyone else
is awake.

Do not speak to me
of reality for I already
know my time here is
limited. I'm trying to
draw out every second
to make it last as long
as possible.

When you remind me
of my humanness— of
my mere lifespan— a knot
forms in my stomach.

Let me pretend
for a moment longer—
that I belong here too.

To Create is to Remember

I look around
and figure this all
might as well be
a mirage, or one
of Morpheus's dreams—
for sooner rather
than later— everything
around me will be
out of reach.

I must be
a special kind
of fool to believe
this feeling of
acceptance
could last.

I feel like I'm lost
in Daedalus's labyrinth
and the winding maze
is my mind.

Every thought leads me
down another dark pathway
and I'm terrified that
when I turn the corner
I will come face to face
with the monster and
the monster will be me.

THE GODS THAT QUESTION ME

They ask me how it feels
to be mortal and I tell them
*I am always restless and
unsatisfied* and they look at me
with envy in their eyes—

they have fallen so
comfortably into infinity
that they have forgotten
what it is like to be
hungry for more time—
to hold someone tighter
because you don't know
if you will ever see them
again and I tell them
that being mortal is terrifying
for each moment could be your
last and they only sigh
and wish they could experience
the vibrancy of a life that is doomed
to end.

To Create is to Remember

Maybe that's the secret—
there is no peace
for the Immortals—
as they are damned
to live forever.

Maybe it would be easier
to rot.

―――◇―――

The burning sun comes out
from behind the clouds— just
for a moment— to cut through
the cold that has seemed to enter
my bones.

―――◇―――

I see Helios from a distance—
he is so often alone.

I wonder if he prefers it that way.

―――◇―――

Atlas is building worlds
again, flower by flower and
sea by sea, and today— the
weight upon his shoulders
doesn't look so heavy.

It turns out— this morning's
rainstorm was no accident.
Circe summoned the clouds.
Each day— she has learned
to harness a new element.

Yesterday— fire. Today— water.
It was only for the minutes when
she was communing— performing
her ancient ritual— that the storm
was overhead. When the enchantress
ceased— the sun returned.

Tomorrow she speaks with the air
so we're expecting high winds.

———◊———

Pan stumbles upon Nyx
as she discovers a nymph
named Echo within the old
stone chapel.

She promises to return to visit
the cursed creature.

*Even though she cannot speak back—
she'll know I'm there,* she told him,
that's what matters.

Holding a griffin
in one's arms is no
easy feat— they bite
and claw and flap
their wings.

I may have ended up
with a few scars on my
arms— but at least the
little creature was sheltered
from harm.

Hecate and Gaia
share wine and bread
by the hearth
as the last speck of
sunlight disappears
from the sky.

I suppose that the
kitchen must be
the most sensible place
for death and life to meet.

The Chronicles of a Mortal in Arcadia

The Immortals are tossing
bone runes to determine
their fates and there doesn't
seem to be any discernable rules.

I rely on the counsel
of Pheobe and Themis
to see me through and hope
that I may make it out
with my destiny still intact.

———◇———

Nyx gains her truest power
at night— and when she tells you
a particular strategy in the games
of the Immortals— it would be
in your best interest to listen.

———◇———

Some people call me a thief,
says Morpheus— as he takes his fill
of the food of the gods— and I wonder
if he means the sweets
or if he means the way
he steals away sleep and implants
the most haunting dreams.

To Create is to Remember

There are seams
in the heavens—
like someone took
a knife to the galaxies
and tried to split them open.

The stars reach toward each other
like a wound trying to heal
and I wonder if the anguish of loss
is the one universal concept
that truly connects
each living being across
the realms of infinity.

CHAPTER FIVE

Hesitation & Doubt

It must have been Morpheus
who convinced me to stay
in the land of dreams—
he's quite the trickster, you see,
crawling through the windows
of your mind all hours of the night.

I wake up groggy, midday— wondering
who I am and where I'm supposed to be.

———◇———

The winds
are blowing
from the east—

Circe
must be
dancing.

The Chronicles of a Mortal in Arcadia

She carries earth in the soles of her feet.
Oceans in her veins.
Atmospheres in her lungs.
Blazing flames in her soul.
She is elemental, a goddess, a high priestess—
but the fearful and foolish
eyes of those who
do not understand
only see her
as witch.
Why must this world condemn those who
could save it?
Do they want to fall apart?
Is it easier to break?

The Immortals gather
round to hear the tales of Atlas—
of the worlds he has made
and those he has only visited.

They hang on every word—
they smile when he smiles
and sigh when he sighs and
I can only hope
that he'll share more stories
tonight.

I tiptoe into Hestia's chambers
to see portals to fantastic worlds
hanging on the wall— and at her
desk— she is coloring her next realm.

I always start with a base of red, she says,
it makes everything warmer.

I think to myself
how lovely a heart must be
to craft worlds where no one
can ever feel cold.

Nike runs by
and I swear— for
a moment— I glimpsed
her wings.

At the court of Demeter—
Hecate offers me ripened red berries
as fresh as the moment
they were picked— I wonder if these
may be pomegranate seeds from Hades—
and I pause with a thought
to Persephone— but with one taste
I can't stop eating— it turns out that
fruits from the underworld
are the sweetest.

The Chronicles of a Mortal in Arcadia

What does it mean— I ask Pan,
to be an Immortal?

He puts down his flute and looks at me,
Even when you're dead and gone—
the concert keeps going.

The Immortals gather
outside for revelry and
merriment— and for a
moment I join them.

A nagging voice creeps
into my mind and I feel
a pain pounding behind
my eyes. It throbs and
overtakes every thought,

You don't belong here, it says—
louder and louder each time. I stumble
away from the table and retreat inside
to the darkened parlor.

You are not one of them— you are
mortal— mere and irrelevant— you are
nothing more than forgettable,
and even if I press the palms
of my hands to my ears and
close my eyes— I can't escape
this violence inside my mind.

Hesitation & Doubt

The Moirai join me
in the dim salon— they
sit across the room— three Fates
so closely tied they could
almost be one woman.

I'm not sure what to say— so
I don't say anything at all.

Birth, Life, and Death—
all right in front of me.

By the time I work up
the courage to speak—
I look up from my feet
and the seat is empty.

The underground caverns
are quieter tonight— most of
the Immortals are sleeping—
Selene was likely the first
to doze off (it is a dark moon, after all)

but I think I like it better this way.
Helios talks of the skies, Pan the earth,
Hecate the underworld, and Morpheus
the land of dreams.

I don't have much to say,
so I just sit back and listen.

The Chronicles of a Mortal in Arcadia

Morpheus begins to spiral— unsure
of what nightmares and dreams to spin—
he claims he's all out of ideas.

Pan takes him by the shoulders and
looks him dead in the eye—
*Stare into the mirror of
who you are and figure out
what you're trying to say.*

I'll return soon, says Helios—
as the void of midnight surrounds us.

I know it is true— but on nights
like this— it always seems like
such a long wait for the sun to rise again.

THE RULES OF ARCADIA
AS TOLD BY RHEA, QUEEN OF TITANS:

— There is stolen lightning in the cellar— do not touch it. It will kill you.
— When propping open the windows, secure them tightly. The Aurai like to slam them closed to watch the glass shatter like ice on the lake.
— Keep the fruit covered, otherwise the furies will swarm.
— The nocturnal flowers need silence to bloom (as they are quite timid) so keep voices down when the sun sets.
— The little griffin demands respect and attention— when spotted make sure to greet him.
— Once a day, in the early evening, the wine spring overflows and spills out into the underground caverns— have your glass bottles ready.
— Demeter's kitchen is the most sacred room in the chateau— always enter with care and leave it better than you found it.
— Take heed when venturing past the golden fields, beyond the bounds of Arcadia— out there be monsters.
— To mark ones time here, one must sacrifice a small piece of ones soul and leave it behind in the Book of Life.
— All that is needed in order to be welcome here is a kind heart, a bit of courage, a fair amount of curiosity, and the sincere desire to create.

CHAPTER SIX

Elysian Fields

Across hills, on this
summer day—
we venture away
from Arcadia.

Come with us, says Calliope,
you won't get another chance.
Beyond the blue iron gate—
we enter Elysium like
feathers on the wind.

The final resting place
of demi-gods— of valiant
warriors and the blessed dead.
Not even an Immortal
is often allowed on the other side of
this barrier— so we take care to tread lightly.

The Chronicles of a Mortal in Arcadia

Winding gardens surround us
and I can hear bells ringing souls
into the afterlife. I look up
to meet the eyes of Kronos—
the god of time. He is the ruler
of this realm— and I've heard
all kinds of terrible stories—
but I suppose half an eternity
has changed him.

Kronos is quiet, and gentle,
and focuses on tending the grounds
more than giving any thought to us.

He isn't so much the ruler
as he is the gardener
of the Elysian fields.

There is a round wishing well
with a crimson-red metal casing
that stands in the middle of the path.

I lean over the edge and
see straight into Tarturaus.

The phrase
be careful what you wish for makes
a lot more sense
when you realize the ones

Elysian Fields

granting wishes are the
devious monsters trapped
in the deepest regions
of the underworld.

Mnemosyne— the goddess
of memory— tells me her secrets
of how she remembers every face
she has ever known (or will know)

and according to her— it is as simple
as putting the face away in the boxes
of one's mind and I don't know how
to admit I've never been good at
organizing my thoughts.

I follow Hecate
through the gardens
of the afterlife and
she introduces me to
flora I could never before
have imagined.

*With the right
kind of care,
she assures me,
flowers can bloom
anywhere.*

The Chronicles of a Mortal in Arcadia

There is a small gate
at the edge of the garden
and I have a feeling
not to get too close.

If I were to approach—
I might be pulled into
the netherworld— lost
between realms.

Gaia shows me
the very portrait
of my creation—
one she crafted long ago.

It's nice to see her
vision of me— and
I hope that the woman I have
become doesn't disappoint
too much.

I've spent
the afternoon
with Calliope

and she's shown me
what it feels like
to dream again.

THE CURSE OF THE GODS

I've come to learn—
being an Immortal
is more of a condition
than it is a choice—

they can't help but
spend their days
in the cradle of creation—
for if they were
to stop— they might
as well rot.

It isn't enough
to simply exist
for all time—

I can see it in their
desperate attempts
to find meaning in all
that surrounds them—
I can see it in the insatiable
passion that burns in their eyes—

the Immortals, more than anything,
just want to feel alive.

The Chronicles of a Mortal in Arcadia

Selene sits beside me—
eyes drooping from
exhaustion. *I'm so tired,*
she says. *Of course you are,*
I think, *it's the middle
of the day.* The moon
shines strongest at night.

Ambrosia, made fresh
by the maenads, is always
hot and ready
for the Immortals to drink—
the only catch is— you
must fight away
the persistent furies.

One thing to understand
about Nyx— she may be
a Titan of the night—
but she despises
walking alone in the dark—
so she *runs.*

I tell you this to ask— next time
you are out in the abyss, feeling nervous,
and you notice her heart racing just as fast—
invite her to walk with you— hopefully,
neither of you will feel so afraid anymore.

Elysian Fields

There is a reverence
in this place— but also
an open door for messiness.

Nothing is sacred— but
everything is holy— in its
own way. There's a freedom
in knowing one is allowed
mistakes— to exist as we are
without the need to appear
mythically perfect.

I have seen Atlas
carry the entire world
on his shoulders and
I have seen him carry
a single flower— both
with the same level
of care and endearment.

I cannot see Lelantos
(for he is the Unseen One)
but I can hear him
just outside Esther's Bath—
he picks a gentle melody
on a guitar— and even
if he is rarely witnessed,
he is welcome— always—
to be heard.

The Chronicles of a Mortal in Arcadia

The furies swarm
the ambrosia— trying
with all their might to taste
a single drop.

I have yet to find my way
to the Court of the Dryads—
but I've heard wondrous tales.

I wonder if mortals
can even enter at all?
Or is it only for
the satyrs and nymphs?

You've heard stories
of Eris as a troublemaker—
but those are all from scribes
and old poets who never knew her.

She doesn't hesitate to say
exactly what's on her mind—
but that bluntness isn't all she is.

I've seen her truly celebrate
those around her,
share music with
the waterfalls, and offer
a safe place to meditate
each evening—

Elysian Fields

inviting all the troubled minds
to breathe in peace and let out
their darkest thoughts
with a healing sigh.

The Immortals
have gathered
around the fire—
just as we have done
since the dawn of
human existence.

For a brief time— it feels
like I belong here more than
anyone else.

Having grown up
with my feet in the dirt
and hands warming—
I attend to these flames
as if they were my own
and at this moment
I am surrounded again—
by mortals.

The Chronicles of a Mortal in Arcadia

By the will of Calliope
I write down
everything I long
to release.
Anxiety,
distrust,
anger—
so much anger.

I throw the spell
into the flames
and it burns like
the very soul of me.

Asteria teaches a game
she learned from the fae—
rhyming and distorting reality
is the object of play with a
strict consequence of hallucinations.

A glass of wine in every hand—
I try my best to keep up— as the
world around me changes shape—
I find myself laughing through my mistakes.

Circe shares with me
her first spell— earth,
water,
fire, air—

Elysian Fields

written in two languages
(only one I can comprehend)
and her words are nothing short
of enchanting.

I can see why the elements
wait for her to speak.

The Immortals burn a star
in the cast iron trough
made by the hands of Hephaestus—
they play their games and
sing their songs and don't even
notice when the fiery orb crawls
over the edge and tries to escape.

Casting itself over the ground
like ink spilling across paper.
They try to stamp it out— to
control it once more— but the
star just wants to be free.

Calliope sings and
we all smile— a gathering
of Immortals— and me,
quietly humming— afraid
to be any louder than a whisper.

But oh— how I long to sing with her.

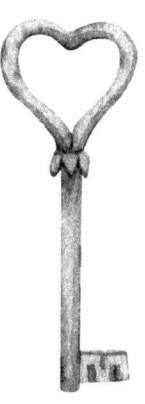

CHAPTER SEVEN

Human & Ephermal

Along this path—
you must take care,
Pan tells me, *for it*
leads far into the wildwood
and if you're not careful
you will fall deep into a well.
The Dryads created it as a trap for intruders.

I find myself hesitating and
gesture to the adjacent path.
He considers it.
This one you may follow
as far as the edge of the world—
so keep your eyes open— for you
could fall right off.

I stand motionless at the crossroads,
Will you tell the trees I said hello? I ask,
a bit too timid to take a step in either direction.

Of course, I will, says the forest god.
With a smile, he takes off down the path
that leads to the end of everything—
without a single fear in sight.

I find Circe— eyes
closed— soaking
in the sun.

She releases
all her thoughts
into a grimoire
by casting
a cleansing spell.

There is something
to learn from
a woman
who takes time
to exist with
and care for
her own mind.

She speaks the
language of Arcadia—
and I wish I could
understand.

Human & Ephermal

The Immortals have all
dispersed to paint and
draw and sculpt the day
to their visions of how
the world is or could be—

and I am left alone to think—

with only the kind maenads
and demi-gods, buzzing around
like bees, and the little griffin
to keep me company.

I would not call him
a king or a ruler— maybe
a leader— but most definitely
a caretaker. Dionysus isn't like
the other Olympians—

he looks us in the eye
and wants us to be there.
Very few from
the outside world
look at those who are
different and truly want to
understand.

The Chronicles of a Mortal in Arcadia

Furies are small
and incessant and
swarm by the dozen.

They may only live for
a single day— but they
spend every minute
of that day being
an absolute terror.

Nyx strolls by
the River Styx
and her reflection
seems more at home
in the dark water
below
than she does
in the bright sunshine
above.

The sirens watch us
as Morpheous and Daphne
lounge with me by the shore
and search for creatures
hiding away in the clouds.

Human & Ephermal

The Aurai gather
around the top of
the waterfall and I watch
as they chase each other
and play among the moss.

When the sun disappears
behind the clouds— they all
disappear too. I suppose
they get cold
in the shadows.

Helios has been gone
for a few days now
and I must say—
we've had more
shade than sun
since then.

―――◇―――

The satyrs are yelling
and roughhousing from
across the lake and I wonder
what kind of games they
might be playing.

Themis takes off with
royal blue wings— passing
through cumulus clouds
and rainbow aureole rings—
determination
in her eyes— a sense
of freedom in her being.

With my feet firmly
on the ground— I look up—
gazing in awe as she soars
across the atmosphere
like a shooting star.

I see the joy on her face
from so far away and
I wish— just for a
moment— I could be
that brave.

Human & Ephermal

I am careful to avoid
the eyes of Medusa as
I traverse Andromeda's
caverns. It breaks my
heart, having to rush
by with my gaze cast
to the ground. I wish
I could look her in the
eyes and tell her, *I know
you're not a monster. You were
hurt. You are still angry.
That's okay.* But instead—
I say nothing at all— and
for that I am ashamed.

When making my way
back to the chateau—
I hear wraiths running through
the woods— I'm too afraid
to look into the void between
the branches— so I turn my head
away and walk a bit faster.

Calliope and Daphne sit
on the stone steps discussing
the art forms of the mortals.

How we dance, how we sing, how beautifully
human and ephemeral we all are—

The Chronicles of a Mortal in Arcadia

only a nymph and a muse
could be so fascinated with
us mortals.

———◇———

An Oread nymph
has come to visit us—

the Immortals gather
around to capture her
form. Every curve is
recorded in graphite,
pigment, and ichor-colored
ink as she holds so still
she could practically be
made of marble.

A part of me wonders
if she is— and when
I learn her true name
is Echo— I realize why
she barely speaks.
She can only repeat, you see,
the last words spoken by another—
this is her curse.

So as some act of kindness
or some sort of understanding—
the Immortals come together
every so often to celebrate her
in silence. To surround her in
appreciation and to make her

feel seen. They turn their sketchbooks around
and circle her in drawings—
showing her the magnificence
we all see.

Even though they are mere echos
of her soul— we all hold onto hope
that they may be enough.

Before she leaves, Rhea says, *thank you.*
Echo smiles and whispers, *thank you.*
I hope she means it.

I am gifted
a fire flower journal
from Asteria and
pine smoke ink
from Circe—
Write what you see,
they tell me, and
I've never felt
more loved as a poet.

The Chronicles of a Mortal in Arcadia

I can't fall
in love with
a god— what
am I thinking?

What is this heart
of mine doing
beating like that?

I know the warning
tales— I've read the
stories— nothing good
ever happens to a mortal
that falls for a god.

Still— I look for you
when I walk into every room.

And suddenly
all I can hear is
your voice from
three rooms away—

and even though I can't
understand every word
you say— I still foolishly
wish it was me to whom
you were speaking.

Human & Ephermal

I hear Lelantos say
how he wouldn't want
to live without Theia
and I feel so selfish.

I've never made anyone
feel that way and I likely
never will. I'm too selfish
with my days. I'm too mortal
to promise this short life
to someone else.

I look in the salon mirror, over
my shoulder, and it is no
surprise that I am only
surrounded by empty air,
voices drifting in from
the other room, footsteps
pacing upstairs— carrying
only a heart, never made for two.

―――◇―――

The wraiths have made it
into the stairwells of Chateau Rouge—

so do not be alarmed if you look back
to see them following you.

The Chronicles of a Mortal in Arcadia

I witness the moment
night and dawn meet
for counsel and advice—
it is Nyx that goes to Eos—
asking her for guidance.

*You must continue to walk
through the darkness to
come out on the other side.*

⸺◇⸺

Morpheus is deep in thought,
planning the newest
nightmares and dreams
he'll create. *They are all
crafted by hand, you know.*

I never realized how much
care and attention go into
each one. Now I feel terrible
for forgetting mine
the moment I wake up.

⸺◇⸺

This is a battle of
knowledge— Phoebe—
wise and level-headed
versus Themis— quick-witted
and clever.
I am careful
to keep out of the way—

Human & Ephermal

I may not know much,
but I am sharp enough
to realize, this is not a fight
I could win if I tried.

Atlas looks at me
and I wonder what
he sees— he once told me
that he can envision
how things go together
and I think that is just
another way of saying how
he can tell at a glance
who around him is broken.

One by one
we say goodnight
and silence falls
til morning light.

CHAPTER EIGHT/NINE

Arcadian Nights

I am awoken
by the mynaeds—
their footsteps
and voices echoing
through the caverns—
all in the language
of Arcadia. I blink
my eyes open and
follow the sound—
they're tending to chores
and singing to themselves.

I can't help but smile
and I wish I could sing along—
but I do not know the words.

They carry fresh linen
in the baskets on their hips and
with laughter and charades,

they tell me of their dreams—
peeling back the bedsheets,
musing they were queens.

There is a wall of roses
outside the caverns
where each Anthousai
has painted a single blossom
her favorite color—
and today the raindrops
are resting on the petals—
making them sparkle
like precious jewels.

If you were to tell me
this is how sapphires
and rubies grow and bloom—
I would be inclined to believe you.

Two young herons
soar through the sky—
feathers of blue— always
two— I wonder where
they come from— I wonder,
can they teach me
how to stay?

Arcadian Nights

He tells me the forest
is quiet— safe— and
a rather good listener.

No wonder he spends
most of his time there.

The River Styx
is changing colors
from midnight black
to turquoise blue and
it must be an abundance
of life seeping in, an influx
of souls that have a
particularly high level of hope.

As the water feeds the shore—
more wildflowers bloom than
I've ever seen.

Maybe all they needed
was something to believe in.

Eros ignores me—
which is not at all
surprising. I've never
been one to catch
the attention of love.

The Chronicles of a Mortal in Arcadia

Damon and Pythias
smile at me quite a lot
and I wish I could
say more than just
a mere hello.

More often than not
I see the goddess
of the moon and
the goddess of the
falling stars
together.

They laugh
side by side
and both seem
to shine twice as
bright.

The Immortals speak
of sending compassion
into the world—

of being like a wave
in the ocean—
nothing more,
nothing less.

They dream of ways

Arcadian Nights

to make those
they care for happier—
and I wish we existed
in a world where
they didn't have to.

———◇———

There's a reason
she's the queen
of the Titans and
five minutes by her
side will confirm
that all the tales
of glory are true.

But what you don't know is—
she loves to wear eccentric
brooches, is modest and
quite shy about her own
creations, and she smiles
in a way that makes you
believe in the most
impossible things.
When she asked me
to speak to the gods— to teach
them— I must admit I wanted
to deny— I was scared out of
my mind— but she made it easy
to believe in myself

so I did it
(even though

The Chronicles of a Mortal in Arcadia

I was shaking)
and in the moments when
I was feeling lost, I'd scan
the crowded room like
a ship searching the coast
for a lighthouse beacon
(or a smile twice as bright)
and without hesitation
she'd lead my thoughts back to shore
and give me the confidence to go on.

Hestia smiles
at me from across
the room and I can't help
but instantly feel
more relief.

Dionysus tells me
of his 100-year plan—
how he wants this place
to be full of a thousand
beautiful things— maybe
even ten thousand.

He chuckles and
shakes his head—
as if the dream is so big
he's trying to shake
some of it out,

Arcadian Nights

like water stuck in his ear—
but the thing is— if he
never had the courage to dream big—
none of us would be here now.

Hecate paints
with sunshine yellow, sky blue,
and rosé wine pink— bringing
bright colors into our lives
and showing us that joy
can be found even in the most
unlikely and brutal places.

I have gone from being
nothing more than
another stranger to
someone to look for
in a crowded room.

Someone to choose.

I don't feel so hesitant
to start conversations and to be
an innate part of this place—
to take up space— to open up—
and let them in.

The Chronicles of a Mortal in Arcadia

There is wisdom in Pheobe
from the ancients— the women
gather around her to learn, to be
understood, to see the world
through new eyes.

She tells me how Jupiter
is ambitious and Mercury
can't stop talking and
that Venus just wants to
love and be loved and
I look at her and think
how wonderful it must be
to commune with the planets—
the giants of primordial beings—
as if they were old friends.

I'm afraid
to tell you
my name.

If you know
who I am—
this all becomes
true.

THE GODDESS THAT KNOWS ME

I have always felt enchanted
by the Dawn— the beginning
of something new—
the promise of another chance.

She sits before me
and pulls another card.
The lovers are in reverse
and neither of us is surprised.
You've been betrayed, she says—
and I think of the man that
destroyed me. *You're exhausted
from something that you aren't
even sure you want*, and I think
of the work that has worn me down
to nothing. *Soon things will change—
your cup will be full once more*, and
I think of the emptiness inside of me—

the stone walls I've built
around that void— to protect it—
to cage me to safety— and I want
to smash those walls down— but
I don't know if I have the strength.

The Chronicles of a Mortal in Arcadia

We were all born
from Chaos— the being
that predated being.
The beginning of
everything— all at once
and yet, so many of us
lose touch— we fall into
mortality and accept it
as all there is.

The monotony of everyday
slowly lulling us into submission.

But some of us are greedy—
we want more— we ache
to taste the infinity
that we were made from.

So we spend our lives
trying to make it back
to the freedom of being
before being— of feeling
everything at once without
shame or apprehension.

Of nothingness and eternity
all at our fingertips.

Arcadian Nights

The Immortals gather
on the floor and suddenly
we are all poets—
trading words and
verses across the room
and I think to myself,

this is what we were
created to do.

Don't look at me
with those eyes—
I don't know what
they mean.
Maybe I'm just
reading between lines
that were never written—
but I feel this shift in energy
whenever you come around
and there's nothing I can do about it.

So I'll just do what mortals
with too many emotions
do best— and ignore them.

So many moons have passed,
Calliope says with a pen
in her hand. *I haven't written
a poem in as long as I can remember.*

This does not stop her
from capturing a moment
and adding a memory and
metaphor to make it something
more, something that will speak
to thousands. How could she
possibly doubt her verses?

These are the words
that will be woven into
the very heart of the universe.

Gold, like ichor, drips
from the walls. The mirrors,
like doorways,
lead to other realms—
each one reveals
another part of who
you are if you dare to
look close enough.

Gilded chandeliers illuminate
the eyes of Immortals as they
laze in the hazy salon— all
draped over velvet chairs
as if they were thrones,
herringbone wooden floors,
tall windows for gazing
at the changing colors of
the sky, and antique tapestries
depicting stories of old.

Arcadian Nights

In the evenings, we gather here
to hide away from the cold—
this is a place I do not feel alone.

I never anticipated
the Fates to bring
us all tea— or I would've
offered to help. She carries
all the cups at once—
as if she had six arms
(and maybe she does)
and then she sits and
contemplates quietly.

I wish I knew the stream
of her consciousness, I wish
I could be courageous enough
to say something more
than just *thank you.*

We are trading poems and
Morpheus is writing for me—
I wonder if he consults
his dreams to find the
words or if he pulls
them from this reality.

The Chronicles of a Mortal in Arcadia

From the breath
of a winding forest—
he wanders out of isolation
to a place where he can
freely create. Hands covered
in charcoal and ink— worlds
brought to life from the
artistic brink between creation
and destruction
he walks the line—
teasing the fall
he holds on—
an impulse
that leads him forward,
held by the hand of
another realm, he follows
that voice deep into the void
to search for the truth
that is scared to emerge—
and on the other side
he shines a stark light
on all our dark thoughts
that hide in the night.

Arcadian Nights

Since my arrival—
half a dozen Immortals
have begun writing poetry
and I can't help but wonder—
are these verses of mine
contagious?

———◊———

Calliope struggles
to finish her poem
and I wish I could find
a way to tell her that all
she has to do
is trust her own voice.

———◊———

The Immortals are dancing
and singing as loud as
they can— the sound travels
through the stones and pierces
the very core of the earth—
quaking the ground
on the other side of the globe.

———◊———

I can't remember
the last time I smiled
so big my cheeks
physically hurt—
I laugh to the point I have to
clutch my sides and

The Chronicles of a Mortal in Arcadia

I don't mind at all
because in this moment—
my pain has never felt better.

I think I finally
got through her
Parian marble exterior—
a tough woman to reach—
I didn't want to give up
on Nike. Maybe all it takes
is someone trying again—
not giving up— saying,
*I will still be here when you
feel ready to open up.*
Maybe all it takes
is patience.

The nocturnal gods
fill the caverns—
belting out loud enough
so the moon herself can
hear their song.

Arcadian Nights

I want to know you—
in a way that I want to
understand the mysteries
of the cosmos— set aside
the dreamy eyes and consider
purely curiosity standing
in front of you.

All I want is every detail
of your soul.

What makes it shine,
what makes it dull, how
does it cope with this
burden of being immortal?

My days are counting down
and I know I'll never truly
be able to leave this place behind.

I carry a piece of everyone
I've known inside of me like a jar
of moments and memories.

I wonder if anyone else will do
the same— or if in a year's time—
they'll all forget my name.

The Chronicles of a Mortal in Arcadia

The stars throw themselves
from the heavens to walk
alongside the Immortals
as they make their way
to their beds in the
darkest hour of the night.

Like little beacons, every god
has a star, and once they make it
to their doors, they toss those burning
creatures back up into the night sky.

Midnights are quiet
in Arcadia— almost silent.
All the birds are sleeping
(even the swifts) and the
rivers themselves seem
to be dozing off.

Like the moon, I can't help
but stay up— staring at the stars,
dreaming of reaching out
my hand and feeling something
other than this cosmic emptiness.

CHAPTER TEN

Intrinsicality

Asteria sings
at dawn—
a soft voice
fading into
the distance—
like stars
that slowly
give way
to daybreak.

Crawling out of bed—
it feels like the covers
are pulling at my feet—
trying to drag me back
into warmth and an
even deeper sleep.
But I fight them off

The Chronicles of a Mortal in Arcadia

like Heracles conquering
the hydra and make it
out the door into morning air
comparable to the tundra—
I will not miss a moment
of this day— not even
for a head full of dreams.

―――◇―――

The scent of lavender
engulfs me and I don't
understand how I ever once
disliked it.

―――◇―――

The mirror begins
to fog— obstructing
my view— and I wonder
if it's Narcissus
from beyond the grave—
trying to save others
from meeting his same fate.

―――◇―――

The furies are drowning
in the whirlpools and
I watch as they climb up
the slick walls— slipping
back towards the swirling depths.

I do nothing to help them.

Intrinsicality

Ever since Helios left—
it's been cold and grey
and gloomy— I hope
he returns today and
that he brings the sun
along with him.

Time is ticking away
and if I can't manage
to earn my immortality—
time will always—
always
be ticking
away.

The edge of Arcadia
is lined in gold— so
if you find yourself
wandering off—
don't worry too much—
there are worse fates than
being lost for all eternity
in a field of blooming suns.

The Chronicles of a Mortal in Arcadia

The mortal boy stares
at me as I walk by
and I wonder what
he's thinking.

I must look a bit
like a fish out of water
and I find myself walking
a little bit faster—
with my eyes cast
to the ground.

A split second later— I hear
Theia's words of encouragement
in my mind— I remind myself
of *who I am* and look up.

I look right back at him, smile,
and offer a wave. He smiles back.

My heart beats a little bit faster—
just enough to remind me it still can.

Intrinsicality

Achilles tells me
I am his heel

and I know—
from now on
a simple *I love you*
will never do.

I draw, paint, write
in ink. Permanent ink.
Sometimes watercolor
pigments— gold specifically.

I make these lines and I have
to commit. I am building
the trust back that was
so forcefully taken away.

One verse at a time—
I am healing.

I can hear Atlas
in his workshop
crafting worlds
from metal and clay.
He wants to make sure
this one has plenty of flowers—
so the mortals
will want to stay.

The Chronicles of a Mortal in Arcadia

The goddesses
are gossiping
in the salon—

their giggling
rings through
the halls and
I sit across
the room,

wishing that I
could trade
secrets too.

———◇———

Rhea sings in the parlor
to a soft, soft, soft guitar
and I slow my breath
to hear her.

The sound of a new song
being written drifts through
the walls and I think of
how lucky I am to
witness the birth of art.

Intrinsicality

The windows are open
and fairies keep stumbling in—
We have to save them!
I rush around the room
to open the doors and
remaining windows—
to give them more chances
to escape. Fairies can't live
for long away from
their flowers, you know.

Pan doesn't hesitate,
he reaches out and
offers his hand—
the fairy holds onto
his thumb and he carries
her out the door.

———◇———

Last night Calliope told me
how she came here to write—

but instead, she has learned
how to see and she can't decide
if it is a curse or a blessing.

Both, I think,
for what a beautiful
and tragic existence it is
to notice every hurting thing.

Like the waning summer moon—
Selene is hard to find and almost
impossible to spend time with.

I know the moon prefers
being alone— but she's fascinating.

I just want to be her friend.

Hecate is draped in white—
she looks like an angel
holding that glass of wine.

The Immortals read their poems
and for a moment they are not gods.

They are defenseless— no armor—
no protection from the outside forces—
barely any skin to shield them.

For a single evening,
we are all as vulnerable
and perishable
as mortals.

Intrinsicality

The Dawn may appear quiet and docile
but I know the truth—
there is a reason we say "the dawn
breaks over the horizon" instead
of tiptoeing or softly shifting
or easily sliding into place
and that is because darkness
must be challenged in order to
be overtaken by light. This leads me
to believe there is no stronger
deity than the goddess that
drives out the night.

Eos stands up to darkness every
single day. She does so by having the
courage to be seen as all that she is.
No hiding. No pretense.
Her bravery can turn even the darkest
of hours into a vibrant sunrise.

The spirits
of the Immortals
are calling and just as Orpheus
taught me, I answer them
in poetry.

I stand to sing my verses
and my heart is trying
to break through my ribcage.
My hands are trembling
and I can hardly breathe.

I want to run away, but
instead, I walk steadily
to the pedestal and pull out
my journal. *I wrote these for you*, I say
and begin to read. I hope they can
see me more truthfully.

———◇———

Once surrounded by only
the unknown eyes
of strangers— I now walk through
this place and I know every
name. I know stories and even
a few secrets. I know fears and
hopes and what their individual
laughter sounds like. Isn't it
marvelous— how we can go
from non-existent to unforgettable
in such a brief amount of time?

———◇———

The room I used
to hide away in— not so
long ago— is now a place
the Immortals gather—

Intrinsicality

so they can stay close.
I never thought my studio
would be a place for anyone
to convene but now it's
the most full room in
the entire chateau and
I have to say— I much
prefer it this way.

———◇———

Hecate grins at me
and kisses Daphne
on the top of her head,
Goodnight, bunnies!

I can't help but be in awe
of how the dark and the light
can exist inside one being
so intrinsically.

———◇———

Morpheus blows smoke
over his shoulder like Absolem—

he leans in to teach his mind games
to the nymphs. *You'll be playing
this in your dreams in no time,* he says.

And something about the tone
of his voice makes it sound
like a threat.

The Chronicles of a Mortal in Arcadia

We gather late
into the night—
the god of dreams
and the god that pulls
the sun across the sky
join me after midnight.

They ask questions
about my mortality—
out of sheer
curiosity— I think—
the bell tolls and
we hear a knock
on the door.

Atlas peeks his head in
and smiles— he has been
working with copper
all day— crafting flowers
for his newest world— and
when he walks into the room
I notice he's lighter— like
a tremendous weight
has been lifted.

He must have gotten
his work done. I'd like
to see the flowers.

Intrinsicality

In a matter of days,
I've gone from being
surrounded in silence
to surrounded in laughter
and I severely prefer
the latter.

The walk back to
Andromeda's caverns
is pitch black and
cold as mid-winter—
but I don't mind
so much
as long as I take
a moment to stop
and look up.

There are so many stars—
I swear I am
making eye contact
with Chaos herself.

CHAPTER ELEVEN

The Immortals

It's half past dawn—
the bells are ringing
and I'm late again.

This feels familiar
but oh— so different—
my lungs still heave
and my muscles still burn
(I'll never get used to this hill)

but something has changed—

I feel *innate*.

———◇———

I walk through
the foyer— my eyes
no longer to the ground—

with every face I meet—
we look at each other clearly.

We see each other completely.

Theia turns around
and looks for her lover—

his hand finds her shoulder—

she feels safe again.

The Moirai ask me
to be the voice of a soul—
a young girl who neither
breathes in this realm
or the next— she could
be entire universes away.

They ask me to
speak her words,
tell her story, recount
her life that may
or may not have
ever happened.

I am honored to be
trusted with a lifeline—
to speak for her in a way,

The Immortals

to allow her to live here
for a day— before
her thread is cut.

The Immortals showcase
their creations and it's plain
to see— bringing something
to life is no easy feat.

I gaze at the room
around me and god—
I want to belong.

I want to feel a part
of something. I am only
scribbled half-poems,
misspelled words, and
a great deal of longing.

Chills run across my body
from a single gust of wind
like a reminder of how fragile
I truly am.

Calliope

It's all chaos, she says
as she explains the
swirling thoughts
inside her mind.

Eyes of unformidable
women cast over all of us
in the ornate room where
the tale of Frankenstein
could have easily been born—

for when this many
creative minds
gather in one place—
there is always
an element of danger.

The Immortals

Pan

Portals into the past—
dark forests and darker
cellars— glimpses into
other worlds.

He captures what captures him.

Every brush stroke
intentional—
not a single one sacred.

He approaches
his paintings
in the same way
he approaches his life—

with a great amount
of thought and not
a single care
in the world.

The Moirai

Telling untold stories— delving into
the subconsciousness mind and bringing
those lost questions to light.

What is obsession and what is love?
What does a woman feel when blindly
following her heart as it leads her
off the edge of a cliff?

What is lost in a world
that dismisses its own
humanity and knowledge
in favor of the ease of
artificial intelligence?
What is gained?

Is it worth it?
Her stories make burning
eye contact— stare us in
the face and ask—
is it worth it?

Lelantos

He has an acute talent for
making everyone around him
feel singular and irreplaceable.

I wish he could view himself
the same.

If I were to call him an artist today
he might try to deny it, but trust me
when I say— he is more artist than
most who claim the title already.

To be an artist is to find beauty and meaning
where no one else can— and no one else
I know can do this quite as naturally as he.

With a guitar in his hands, he strums,
claiming it's just something he does
to pass the time—
and it's silly because without
even realizing it— he might
be the truest artist of us all.

Phoebe

She casts her eyes
upon everything—
everyone— as a possibility.

She finds beauty in anything
from fields of sunflowers
to crimson red tractors.

To her— the pen is
a meditation— watercolor
a haven. Each day she paints
her own sanctuary and
we must all be grateful—

for she has chosen to share it.

The Immortals

Gaia

She's a giver— she always
has been since the dawn
of everything. Fascinated
with windows into the soul—
she finds inspiration in
the world around her
and invites it inside
to settle in and be cared for.

She longs to give— to
communicate— to stop
and say, *I can see you, you can see me—*
I want to understand you,
do you want to understand me?

Selene

She shows us memory
and liminal spaces— collecting
objects that make up
the background of our lives.

She is gentle. She is quiet—
she feels aggression
in old lace— a less precious
approach to life— and yet—
she captures a soul so completely.

Even (especially) the souls
that have long since passed.

Eos

She wields every color
of the rainbow and covers
her chest in pigment— declaring
herself as a work of art.

She speaks of how
she has spent a lifetime
learning how to accept herself
at all— learning how to boldly
show up as all that she is— with
no more shame.

She is showing me—
by example—
what it means to
embrace individuality.

Hecate

She sees the world in a way
I will never be able to myself—
in bold shapes and sunshine colors.

If you look long enough— her art
begins to sing. She carries her spirit
outside her body and fills
the room with bright energy.

And when she looks at you—
you can't help but believe
in the allure of the unexpected too.

Asteria

They have secrets—
I'm sure of it.

Prussian blue,
cadmium yellow,
permanent red,
the faces of
the unknown—

who know more
than they'd like to say.

And maybe they'd
never tell us in
the first place—
even if we asked
nicely.

Helios

To capture the world
is to understand it and
as he delves deeper
into the landscapes
that surround him
and focuses in—

everything else fades
to blur and I imagine—
in the end— he comes
to understand
himself more too.

Morpheus

Gazing into
another realm
and bringing it back
to this one—
I wonder if he
is disappointed.

That even if this world
makes more logical sense—
does his alternate reality
offer more understanding?

I wonder— if one day—
we'll lose him
to that place
completely.

Circe

Bells ring and
a swift circles overhead
like a blessing.

An alter to the elements
is illuminated by
the afternoon sun—
and so is she.
The song of a dying rose.
A woman on a path
of remembering her origins—
of the universe
that is woven
into her veins—

she dances
and her soul converses
with the cosmos.

Themis

She is made of
summer skies—

the light pours
out of her when
she feels safe,
I can feel it
in the colors
that surround us—

like an aureole, she is
bright and unexpected
and divine.

She has known darkness
in her time, it's true—
but today— her starry eyes
shine celestial blue.

The Chronicles of a Mortal in Arcadia

Atlas

He longs to reach
through time—
to bring a new hour
upon nature and
create a mark that,
contrary to most,
will not and should not
last forever.

His creations may
take centuries to
turn to dust— but
as all things must—
one day— they will be
as far gone and loved as
the rest of us.

Nike

She feels nostalgia
in doorways and
deteriorating buildings
and captures them
while they are still here.

She feels their impermanence
the way she feels her own.

Nothing lasts forever—
and she is acutely aware
that time is limited and
we only have so many
chances to truly *see*
when looking at the
vast world that
engulfs us.

Hestia

She wishes to bring warmth
to this world and I hope
she knows that *she* is the warmth.

In the way she says,
you are so brave,
makes me believe
that maybe there is still
kindness in the world
so big and genuine
that we might just be saved
after all.

Nyx

Music rings through
the cold rooms and
she says, *just stay down.*

These words are meant
for anyone who
oppresses others.

Joan of Arc once walked
the paths of Arcadia—

we stand before
a phoenix rising—
but the difference in her is—
she does not rise only
for herself. With her bold fire,
she is orchestrating
a woman's uprising
to span across the realms.

She is teaching us
how to burn— together.

Eris

She carries realms inside her,
novels of conflict and resolution—
oceans of knowledge on
the most obscure things.

She weaves in all that she knows
to create a world unto itself—
after fourteen years—
finally complete.
Bound in thread and glue and
linen and leather—

a piece of her very essence
lies in every page—
to continue to tell
her stories even
long after
she fades away.

The Immortals

Mnesomyne

Capturing figures
like genies in lamps—
these Dryads and Naiads
are clearly not trapped.

They flow through color
as water flows in the River Styx.

In her hands Oreads
will never be chained down—
in her queendom— the nymphs
are free.

Theia

Flowers encircle her
and french blue
covers her— she sees
the world in colors
I never knew existed.

She contains a passion
that radiates
brighter than Polaris—
and it acts as a similar
kind of beacon—

calling lost souls
to a brighter world.

Daphne

Her art touches others, deeply.
It makes them feel known, feel
seen, feel something more than
just the ache of every day
mediocrity.

She helps others trust in the
wonder of life— to seek it out
for themselves.

Her art makes this world
a more bearable place and
no one else in the entire
fabric of time
could create exactly
as she does.

Her art is meant to be shared.

I only wish she could
believe it herself.

CHAPTER TWELVE
Of the Soul

The Immortals have donned
costumes of mortals and
they dance and sing
all around me.

I am clothed in
a floor-length cape
fit for a queen.

I twirl around, smile,
and sing as loud as
my lungs allow and
suddenly I can't feel
time passing— I can't feel
the grief, dread, anger, or
mortality in my bones
any longer. I feel as though
I could live forever.

The Chronicles of a Mortal in Arcadia

Eris dances in the rain
and for a moment
all her walls are washed away.

———◇———

The Fates
are wearing
angel wings.

———◇———

Calliope takes the floor
and we all can't help
but stop and watch as
the muse fills the room
with her song.

———◇———

The moon
is singing now—
and I've never
before seen
her shine
so completely.

———◇———

Pan and Nike sway—
Mnesomyne dances
with Calliope— Helios
blocks my view
(it would be the sun

Of the Soul

to blind my eyes)

Daphne twirls in
the night sky with
Asteria and Selene.

Themis sings as loud
as she can and Atlas
smiles at me.

Chateau Rouge is filled
with music, dancing,
laughter and rooms full
of grateful hearts—
just as it's meant to be.

I stare out the window
into infinity— some may
call it the void but I call it
possibility. Darkness is
an invitation for light
to shine— and to shine
at its very brightest—
for it is only in
the deepest parts
of the unknown that
anything worthwhile
can be discovered.

My name
was chosen
for me
long ago—

I didn't know
how to accept it
until now.

A butterfly lands
on my palm and
she stays.

I stand by the
open window,
and she shows me
who I am meant to be.

This creature
is my immortality
and she stays.

The winds blow
across me like
a breath of
everlasting life—

Goddess of the soul,
it whispers, *do not
be ashamed.*

*Psyche, it is time
to tell them your name.*

CHAPTER THIRTEEN

Prophecies

The sunshine
has returned
just in time for me
to say goodbye.

The winds called Boreas
blow in from the north—
leaves tumble away
from the village and
sooner than I would like—

I know I'll have to follow.

I happen upon Calliope
in a circle of salt—
a single candle burning

The Chronicles of a Mortal in Arcadia

in the center. She faces
the waxing moon and
does not notice me.

Hecate chants and instructs her—
something magical is happening.
I sneak by and slip into
the chateau by way of
the towering front door—

I look over my shoulder
and see them embracing
each other. There is
so much power
in womanhood.

The Immortals come to me,
one by one, to ask for
their prophecies.
I was trained as
an oracle, you see,
and with permission
from those who seek
poetry— a measure of
truth may be foretold.

As Selene sits across
from me, I ask to
see her soul.

A PROPHECY FOR SELENE

Some may say synergy
is the ultimate goal—
to mesh in the flow
of all that surrounds you—
to practically lose yourself
as the single tree in a vast forest—
to be so engulfed by sameness
that you cease to carry
the burden of individuality.

But my darling— this is not
the only path— for the red forest
is releasing you— like the
autumn leaves that fall from
the oaks and maples— to emerge
from these winding woods and
grow wings of your own.

To take a risk, to fly higher
than anyone ever thought you could.

To be illuminated by the bright sun,
just as you've always been meant to—

some people are made to fade into
what others see as acceptable—

but please know— dear one—
you are not one of them.

A PROPHECY FOR MNESOMYNE

Roots that reach deep
into the earth, sun above
and a burning core below—
she stands tall and reaches
for the sky wondering
what the world would be like
from a bird's eye view—

what it would be like to fly—

and as her eyes cast across
the clouds she thinks that
maybe she already can.

Maybe true sanctuary is found
within our bones— so that
anywhere we go can become
a place of creation and understanding—

and as the sun travels the sky
and melts into the dark of night—
she smiles— for the stars always
shine brighter when she
needs them the most.

As the moments around her pass,
she gathers memories in jars— storing
them forever in the corners of her heart.

A PROPHECY FOR THEMIS

She has known grief— as if
it was created inside of her
from the very beginning—
she has also known anger
and sadness and determination
and above all, she has known love—

this needle of a compass that
points her forward, some days—
the direction is one she doesn't
want to follow— for often the path
is one she must walk alone.

And I wish I could tell her
of the lotus— how no other flower
on earth blooms through the mud
and spreads its petals so beautifully.
So bravely. How when I look at her
immersed in music— I see the same.

I see someone beautiful. I see
someone brave. I see someone
ready to bloom.

A PROPHECY FOR CALLIOPE

From a time of focus— a time
of working— years of short days
and long nights— time itself seems
to have been moving too fast.

I know it's hard to hold— damn near
impossible— but my darling— you are
not meant to reach out and grasp every
moment— for the minutes will pass
regardless of whether we notice the stars
shining or not. A circle of salt— a single
candle beneath the moon— a connection
to ancestors that seem to speak through you—
to tell the forgotten stories of those
nobody cares to remember— to carry
a torch inside of you for every invisible woman.

Know that your flame will never go out—
for you are meant to shine a light on the voices
that have been lost to our universal fight.

A PROPHECY FOR ATLAS

Every storm must come to an end, they say—
but this must be from those who have
never stood out in the pouring rain
for years on end with no front door
to walk in. Maybe the storm isn't something
you can escape— but something you must
learn to carry with you— as the skies clear
above— thunder bellows inside your head
and I know you try to ignore it— but darling—
you must stop all that.

It is no cowardly retreat
to long for a sanctuary—
to search for a home.

Focus in— hold lightning
in your hands (even if it burns)
and forge a new path.

Some people follow roads
that others have carved—
you were created to
craft your own— even if,
for now, you must do so alone.

A PROPHECY FOR NIKE

From generations
of walking alone—
of the past that echos
through time— she carries
possibilities in her hands
like seeds. Protecting them
through the harshness of winter
and waiting for spring— for
warmer days are coming
and she just has to believe—
trusting in the changing
of the seasons, the winds,
in the way she has learned
to trust in herself— she
plants the seeds and cares
for them ever so carefully—
and as the dreams begin
to sprout— she looks up
right as the sun breaks
over the horizon—
a promise of a new day,
a new beginning,
a garden (a life) of vibrant blooms.

A PROPHECY FOR EOS

An ever-flowing river carries her,
from one year to the next—
as the days drip down
the outside of the window
she watches the rain
and dreams of far off worlds.

Floating through the sea
is a lot like flying, but with a
more determined direction—
be careful not to force
the hand of the river too much or
one may end up in uncharted waters.

Danger lies in the storms that
surround her mind but it is
what waits on the other side
that makes it all worth it.

Keep dancing to the sound
of the thunder, brave one,
for the crackling of the sky will
soon sound as sweet as a bell ringing.
In the meantime, release control
to the waves— and know that soon,
stillness will be yours once more.

The Chronicles of a Mortal in Arca

You're made
of butterflies,
Theia tells me.

She can
see right
through
my skin—
as if it was
transparent—
straight through to
my winged soul.

*You're tough
and confident
on the outside,
but so fragile
on the inside.*

Morpheus says
he doesn't want
the night to end
and only a god of
dreams would be able
to control that.

I wonder if the sun
will come up at all
tomorrow.

Prophecies

Gaia closes her eyes
for an instant and
the whole world stops
spinning until she's ready
to open them again.

I say goodnight
to the brightest star
in the sky and she
holds me tighter—

I don't want
to wake up tomorrow
to take only her
memory with me—
and yet I have no choice.

The Immortals gather
at the edge of Arcadia—
where the suns and stars
are grown and harvested.

One day— they will
be put into the night sky
to form new constellations
for faraway worlds.

But for now, they shine only for us.

The Chronicles of a Mortal in Arcadia

The hand of god
is summer sunlight
and we are all touched
by the divine.

———◇———

The Immortals weave
through the fields of stars
at the outer bounds
of this realm.

They move confidently—
unafraid of being burned
at a single touch.

I stand back— longing
to dive in. My feet never
move forward.

The Chronicles of a Mortal in Arcadia

My days here were
always numbered—

for the mortal
world is in desperate
need of poetry.

I watch them in
the distance
wading through
the golden stars.

They skip
and dance
and run and
they trust
themselves
implicitly.

I tightrope on
the border of
Arcadia, knowing
these are my final
moments here.

In my time
among gods
there is one
key truth
I have learned—

Prophecies

the only thing
holding me back
from eternity
is myself.

There is no one
in this realm or
the next who can
tell me what I'm worth—

only I can declare myself
an *IMMORTAL*.

And if there is one thing I am now
most sure of in all the world—

I am meant to be an *ARTIST,*
evermore.

Epilogue

A goddess of the soul—
I am called Psyche.

My butterfly wings
are brimmed with dew,
brand new, and I'm still
learning how to fly.

Luckily— I've never been
too afraid of heights.
You might have heard
my story before— but like with
so many myths— you haven't
been told the whole truth.

This eternity I've claimed is not
for *me* to experience. It's for you.

I earned this artist's immortality for *you*—
whoever is reading these words.
May you continue to return to these poems
long after I've turned to dust.

My voice, my poetry, my artistry
lives on— forever— in your hands.
Thank you for holding
my fragile soul in your palm.

Thank you for keeping me alive.

Dragonfly wing

Aurai wings

Ambrosia

ACKNOWLEDGEMENTS

To Beulah & Ziggy— thank you for creating this heaven on earth for artists, and for allowing a wistful poet like me to visit and reignite my imagination & voice.

To Laura— thank you for being my forever best friend.

To Kristine, Jonathan, Mike, Greg, Erin, Brandon, Leigh, Celine, Leah, Evan, Jen, Jacqui, Victoria, Libia, Sonja, Kat, Monica, Christina, Lauren, Michelle, Alison— thank you for opening your hearts so quickly and completely to myself and each other. In a short time, we became such a singular menagerie of artists. Our days together were unforgettable and I hope they'll always be remembered well in these pages. From strangers to lifelong friends, I adore and cherish each and every one of you.

To Marie, Remy, Angus, Roma, Coco, Quentin, Lorine, Lydia, Lara, Matthew, Netta— thank you for taking care of us, creating art with me, and providing such a welcoming enviroment for each artist to be their authentic self.

GLOSSARY OF GODS

Rhea - Titaness Queen of the Gods
Dionysus - Olympian god of wine, festivity, and patron of the arts

---

Daphne - A Naiad nymph of the River Ladon in Arcadia
Theia - Titan goddess of sight and the shining ether of the sky
Morpheus - The son of Hypnos and god of dreams
Lelantos - Titan god of air and the unseen
Pan - The god of shepherds, hunters, and the mountain wilds
Asteria - Titan goddess of falling stars
Atlas - Titan god of astronomy who bore the sky aloft
Nyx - Primordial goddess of the night
Selene - Titan goddess of the moon
Mnemosyne - Titan goddess of memory and remembrance
Helios - Titan god of the sun
Gaia - Primordial goddess of the earth
Hestia - Olympian goddess of the hearth and home
Circe - Enchantress and goddess of sorcery
Eos - Titan goddess of the dawn

Nike - The winged goddess of victory
Eris - The goddess of strife, discord, and rivalry
Calliope - The eldest muse and goddess of epic poetry
Pheobe - Titan goddess of intellect and prophecy
Themis - Titan goddess of divine law and justice
Hecate - The ancient goddess of magic, spells, and witchcraft
The Moirai - The Fates, the three goddesses of fate who personified the inescapable destiny of man
Psyche - Mortal transformed into immortal goddess of the soul

---

Demeter - Olympian goddess of the harvest and agriculture
Hermes - Olympian herald of the Gods and god of travel
Eros - Olympian god of love
Damon & Pythias - A pair of mortal friends who symbolize trust and true friendship
Demi-Gods - A part mortal and part divine being.
Maenads - The attendants and priestesses of the god of wine
Cadmus - Demi-god of alphabets and writing
Echo - An Oread nymph and the goddess of echoes
Achilles - A hero and known as the greatest of all Greek warriors
Charon - The ferryman who transports souls to the underworld
Zeus - Olympian King of the Gods
Kronos - Primordial god of time and king of the Titans
Chaos - The first entity to emerge at the dawn of creation

Arcadia - In mythology, Arcadia is a mysterious place, full of mythical creatures such as nymphs, muses, centaurs, and legendary gods and goddesses. Old tales describe Arcadia as a true heaven on earth.

Immortals - In mythology: supernatural beings, deities, undying creatures. In this story, the Immortals are artists.
Primordials - The first and oldest generation of gods
Titans - The former gods, the generation preceding the Olympians
Olympians - The twelve major dieties of the Greek pantheon
Aurai - Nymphs of the breezes
Naiads - Nymphs of rivers, lakes, fountains, and springs
Dryads - Nymphs of the trees
Anthousai - Nymphs of flowers
Oreads - Nymphs of mountains, caves, and grottos
Zephyr - The god and personification of the West wind
Boreas - The god and personification of the North wind
River Styx - The main river of the Underworld that Charon takes souls across to enter Hades
Hades - The underworld
Tarturus - A deep abyss and prison for the Titans
Daedalus's labyrinth - The maze designed by Daedalus, the father of Icarus, to contain the Minotaur
Ichor - The golden blood of the gods
Ambrosia - The food or drink of the gods that is said to grant immortality or longevity to those who consume it
Furies - Chthonic goddesses of vengance
Narcissus - A beautiful hunter who fell in love with his own reflection & perished tragically
Heracles - A demi-god son of Zeus with divine strength
Orpheus - A demi-god and renowned poet and musician
Persephone - Goddess of spring and Queen of the Underworld
Andromeda - An Aethiopian princess renowned for her beauty, offered as a sacrifice to Poseidan's sea monster and saved by Perseus, a legendary Greek hero. After her death, she was transformed into a constellation.

THE ARTISTS

Château d'Orquevaux - @chateau_orquevaux

Laura - @l.a.clift
Kristine - @kristineballard_artist
Jonathan - @jonathanchen.art
Greg - @megamuppet1
Erin - @erinharman.art
Brandon - @adventureswithjolly
Leigh - @leighbrooklynart
Celine - @celineelizabethart
Leah - @leahmarianiartspace
Evan - @evangoldmanart
Jen - @jenniferlynnbeaudet
Victoria - www.risetoritual.com
Libia - @mexican_haiku
Sonja - @sonjaholmbergartwork
Monica - @missmmccarthy
Christina - @christinawald_art
Lauren - @crafty.lo
Michelle - @michellemulletart

ABOUT THE AUTHOR

At the edge of Arcadia

Rachel Clift is a poet, artist, & traveler based in the mountains of East Tennessee. More than anything— she longs to inspire people. This is her eighth book and first fictionalized memoir written in poetry— created over the course of two weeks at the Château d'Orquevaux Artist Residency in the summer of 2023.

She is a firm believer that traveling with only a backpack and little to no plans is the most marvelous thing one can do and no matter how many times a heart may break— it will always keep beating.

RCLIFTPOETRY.COM @R.CLIFTPOETRY

www.ingramcontent.com/pod-product-compliance
Lightning Source LLC
Chambersburg PA
CBHW050731010526
44107CB00009B/813